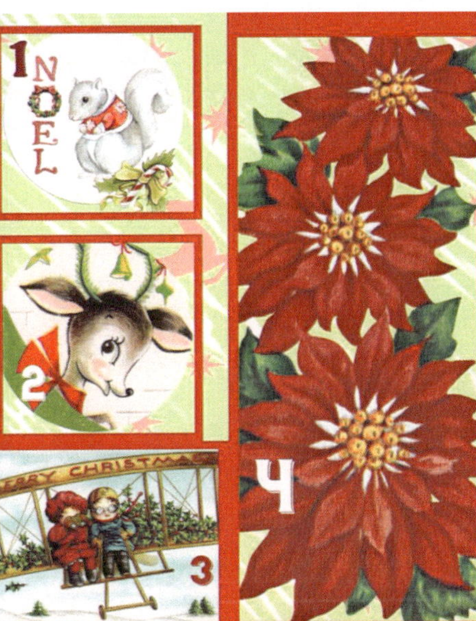

1
NOEL
2
MERRY CHRISTMAS
LOOKING FOR SANTA
3

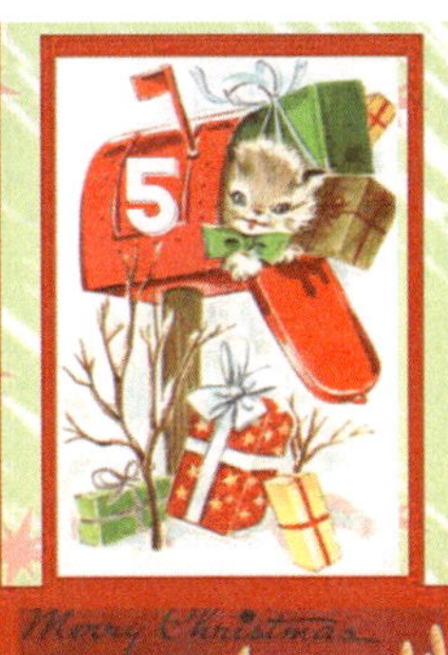

5

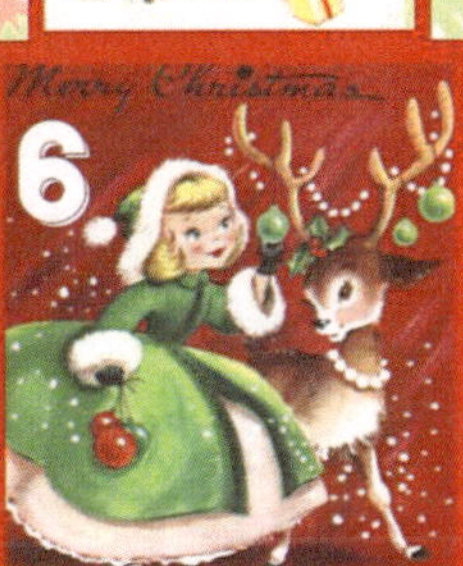

Merry Christmas
6

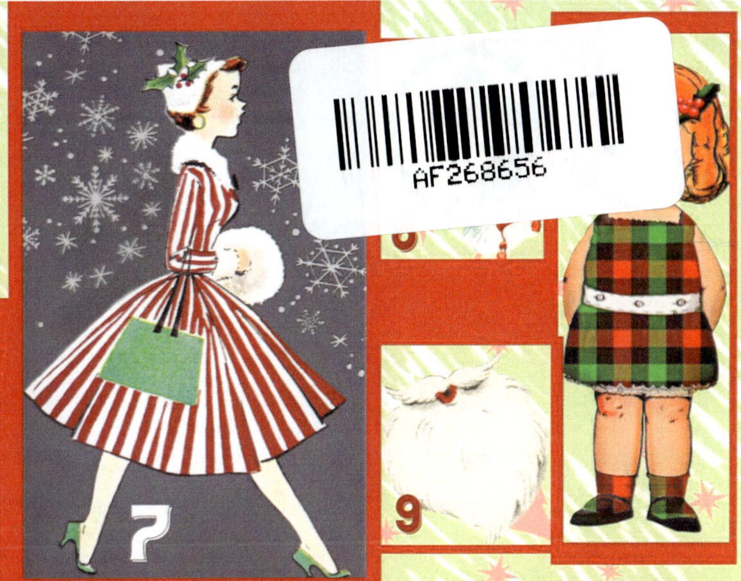

7

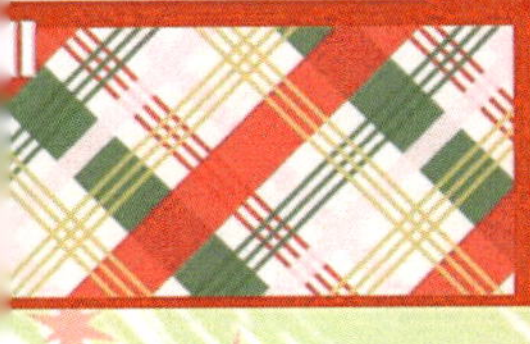

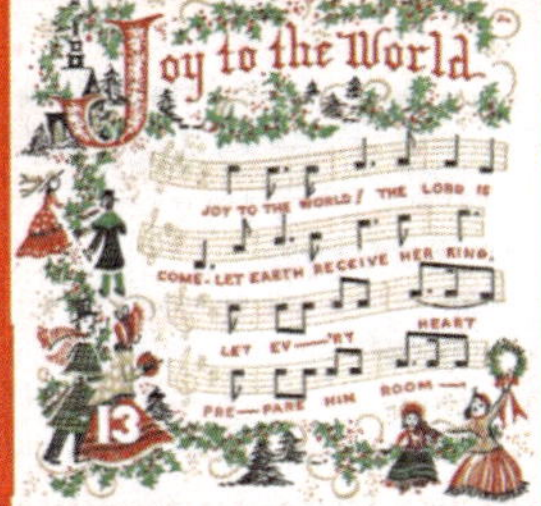

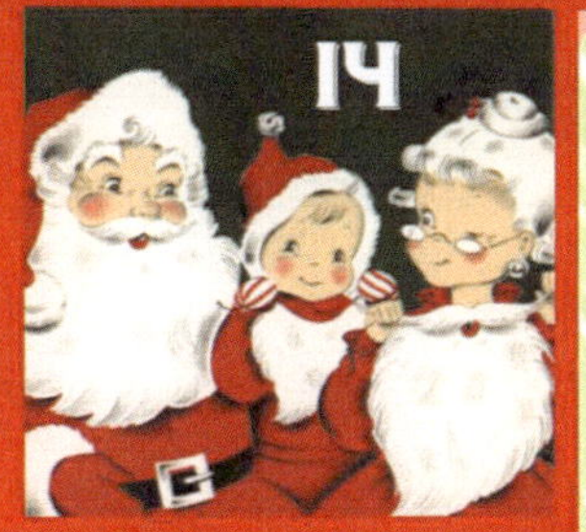

Joy to the World
JOY TO THE WORLD! THE LORD IS
COME. LET EARTH RECEIVE HER KING.
LET EV-RY HEART
PRE-PARE HIM ROOM
13

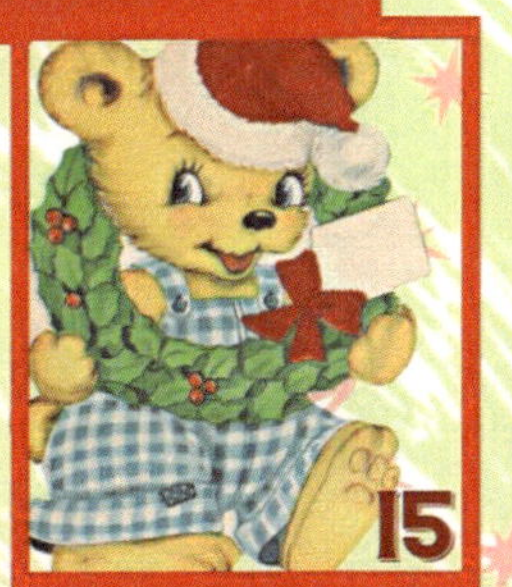

14

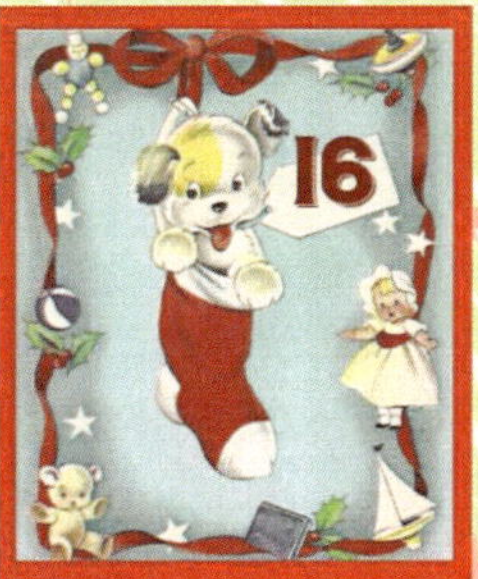

15

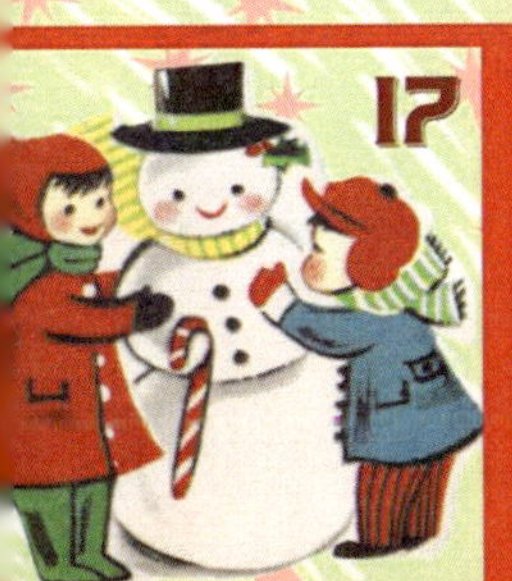

17

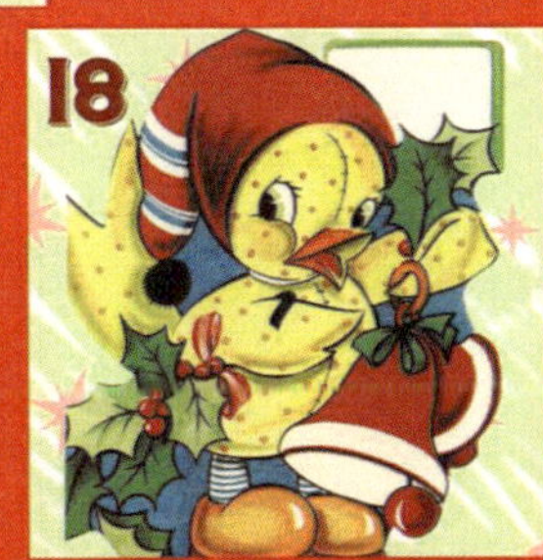

JOY
12

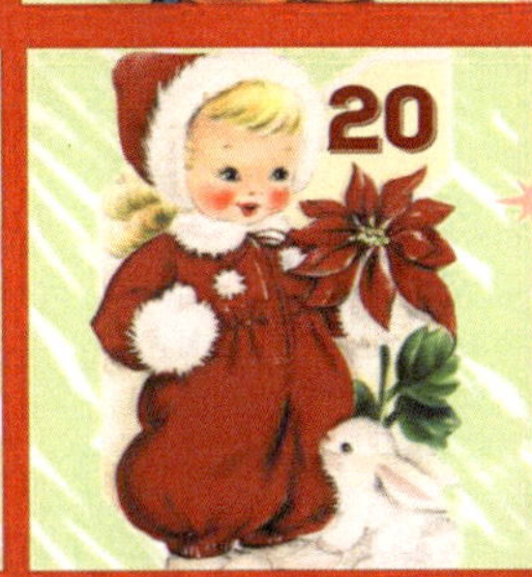

19

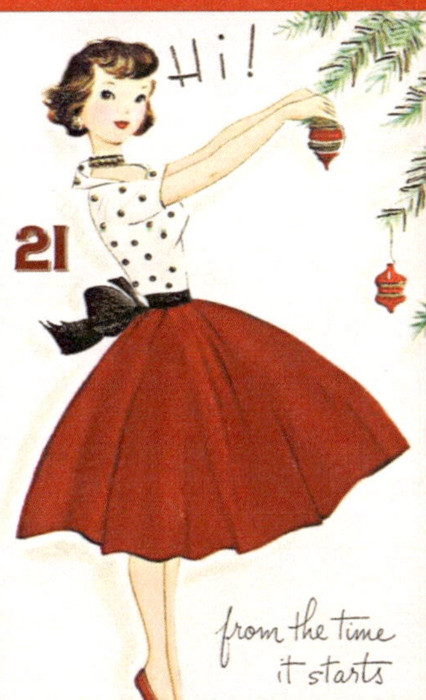

Hi!
21
from the time
it starts

22

23

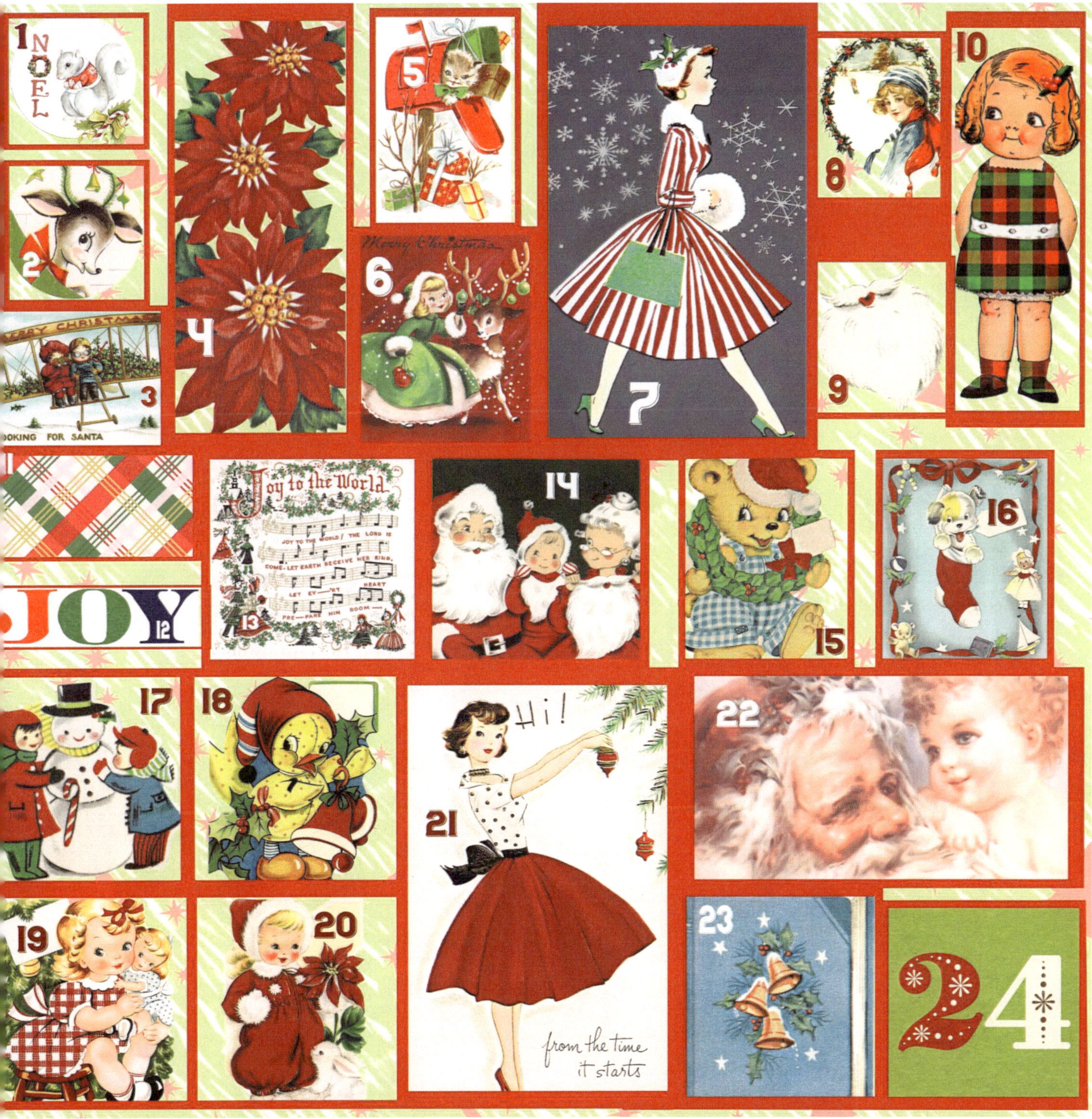

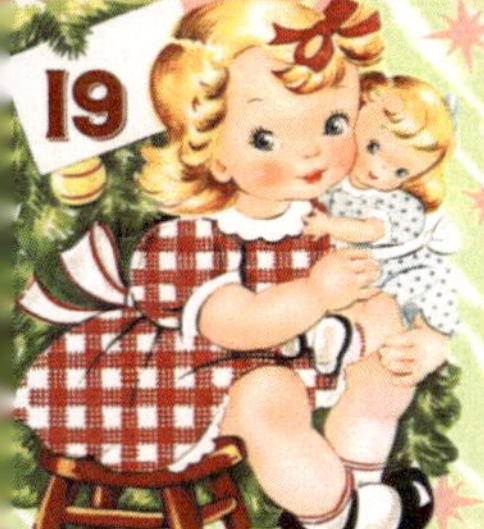
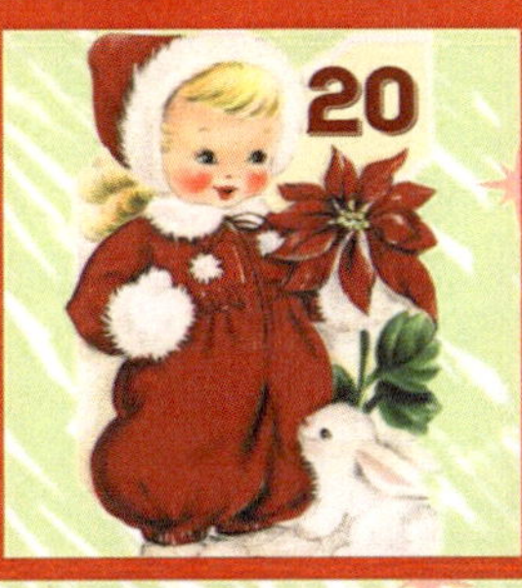
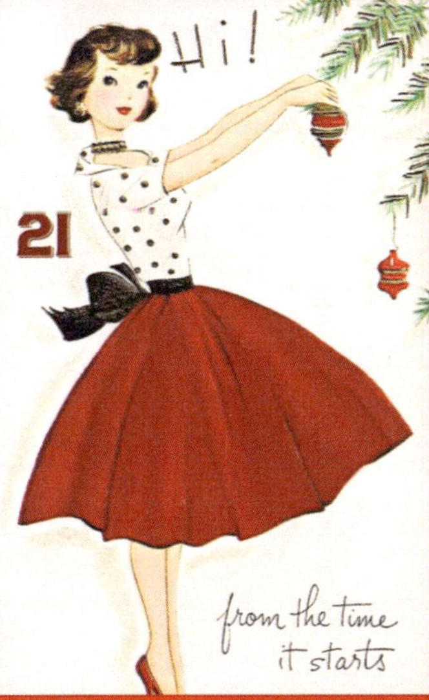

NOEL
LOOKING FOR SANTA
Merry Christmas
Joy to the World
JOY TO THE WORLD! THE LORD IS
COME - LET EARTH RECEIVE HER KIND,
LET EV'RY HEART
PRE-PARE HIM ROOM
JOY
Hi!
from the time
it starts

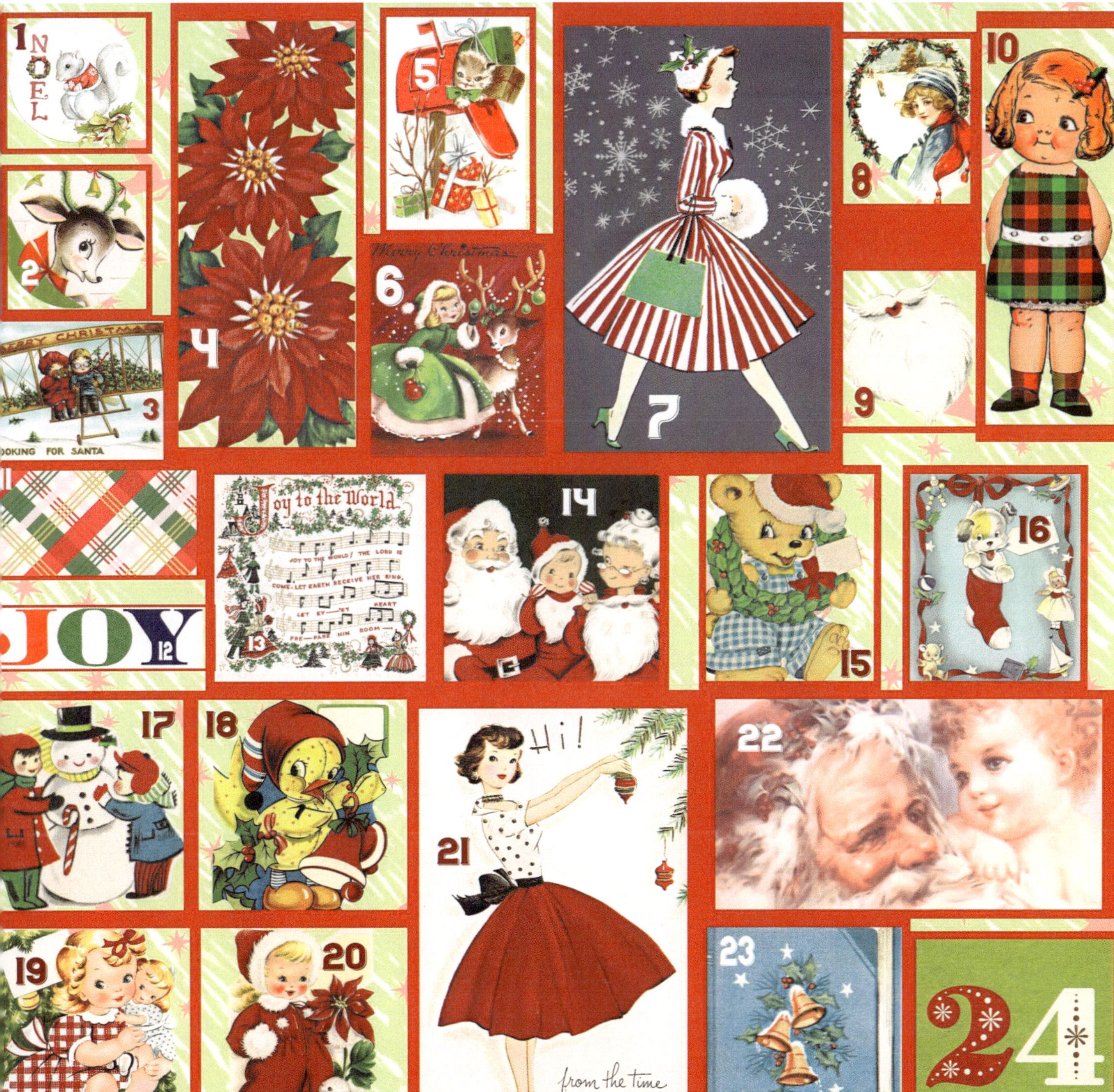

1
NOEL
2
MERRY CHRISTMAS
3
LOOKING FOR SANTA
4
5
Merry Christmas
6
7
8
9
10
JOY
12
Joy to the World
JOY TO THE WORLD / THE LORD IS
COME · LET EARTH RECEIVE HER KING,
LET EV'RY HEART
PRE-PARE HIM ROOM
13
14
15
16
17
18
19
20
Hi!
21
22
23
24
from the time
it starts

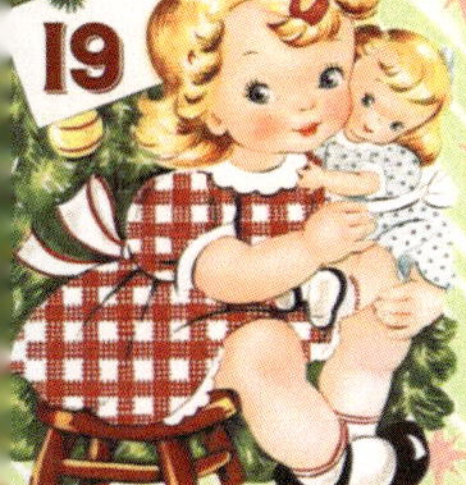
19

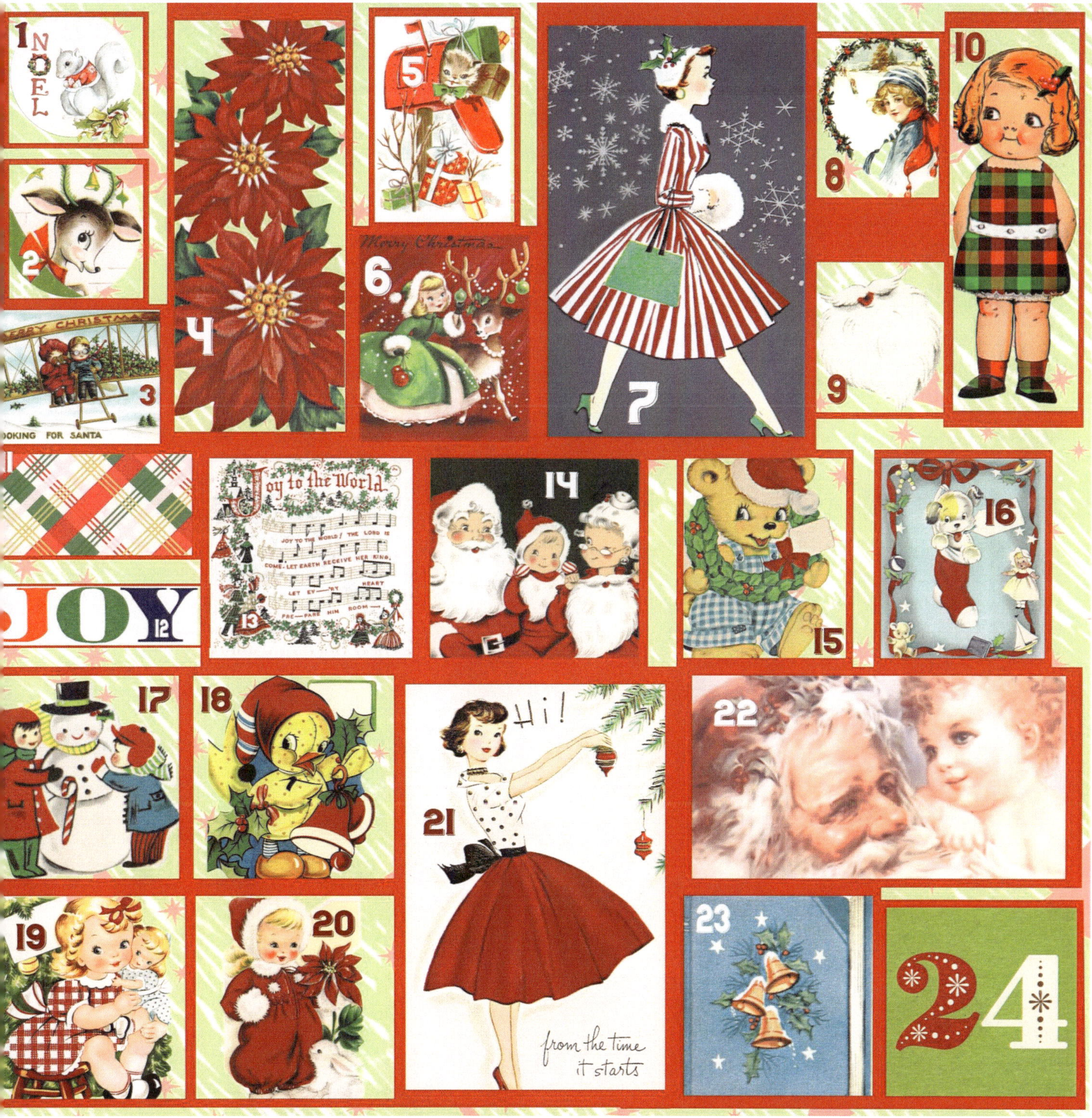

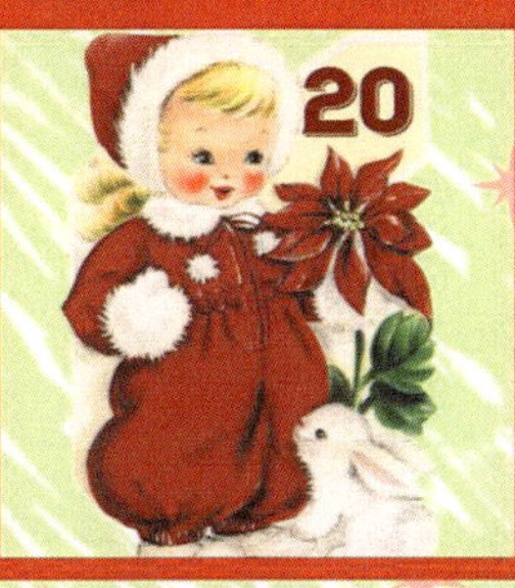
20

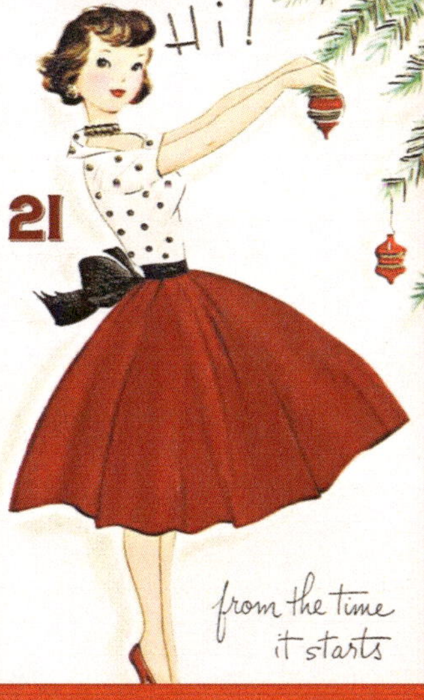
21
Hi!
from the time
it starts

22

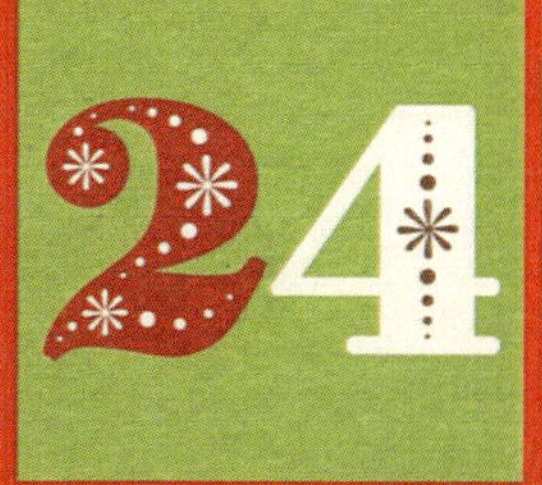
23
24

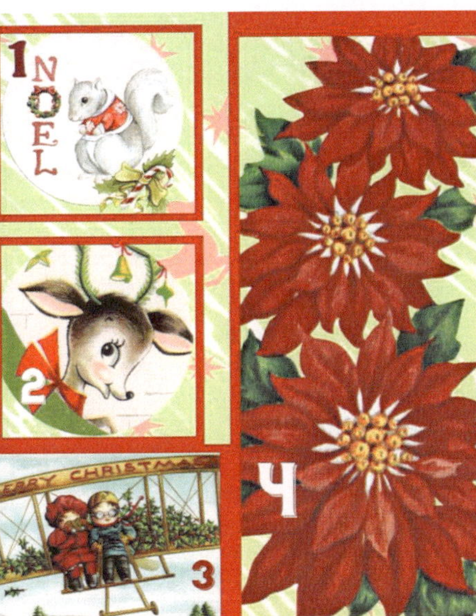
1
NOEL

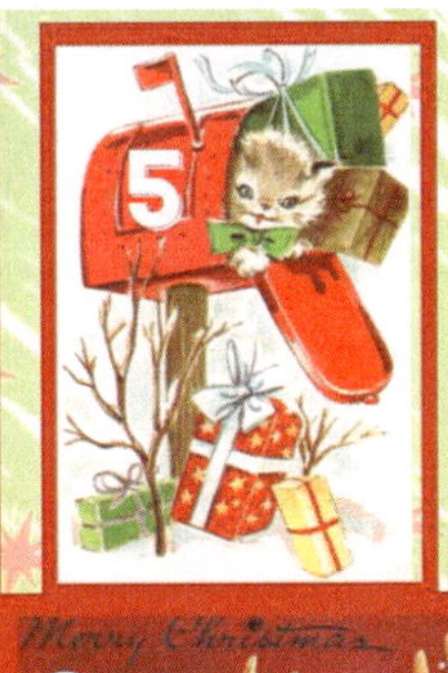

ERRY CHRISTMAS
3
OOKING FOR SANTA

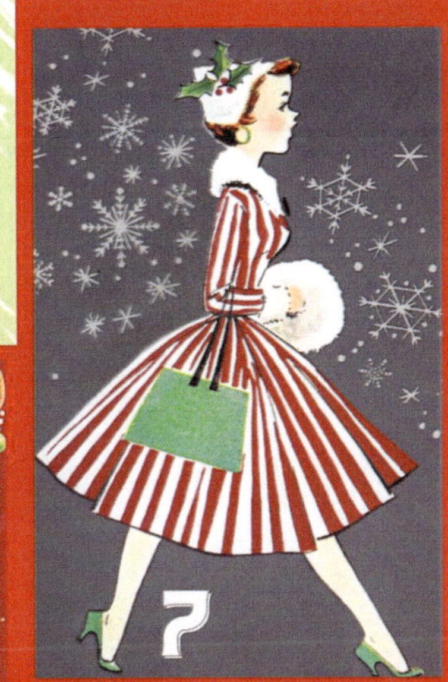
4

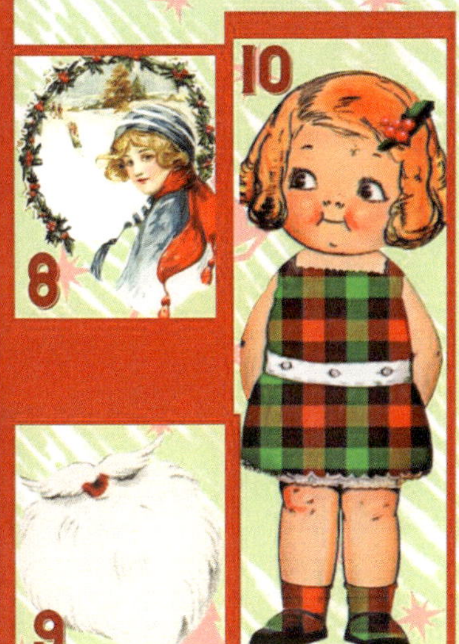
5

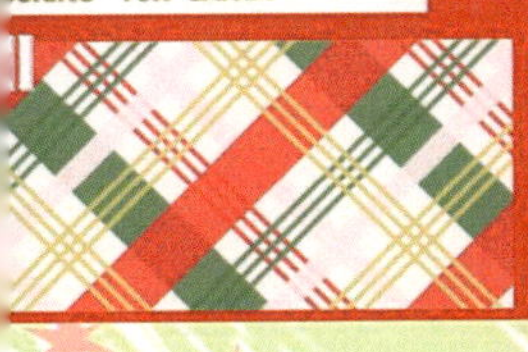
Merry Christmas
6

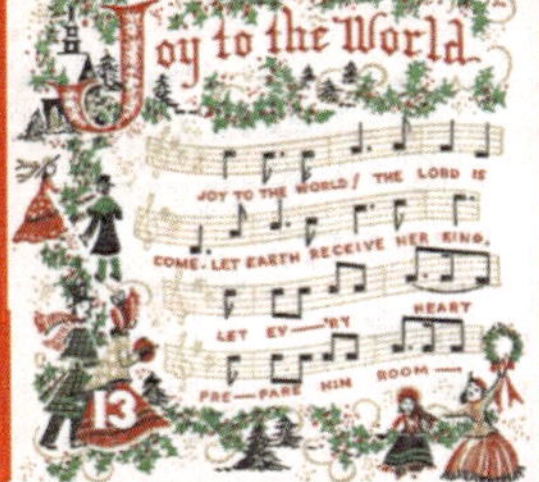
7

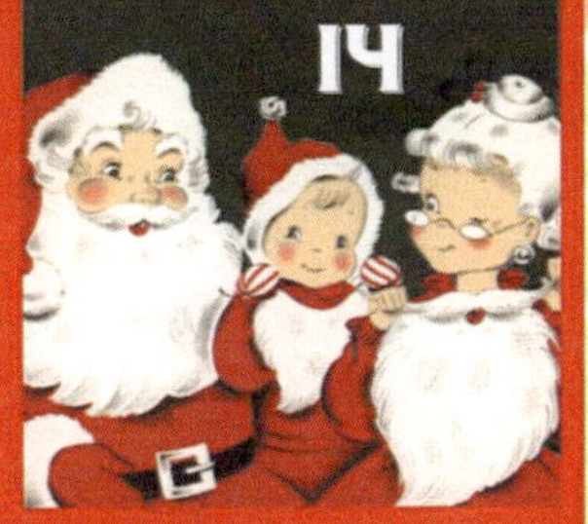
8

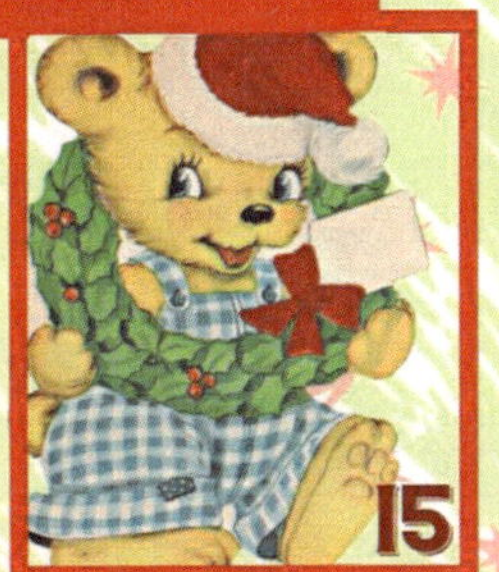
9

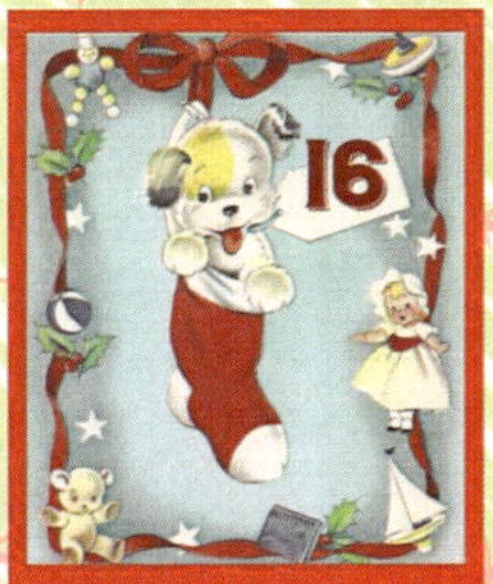
10

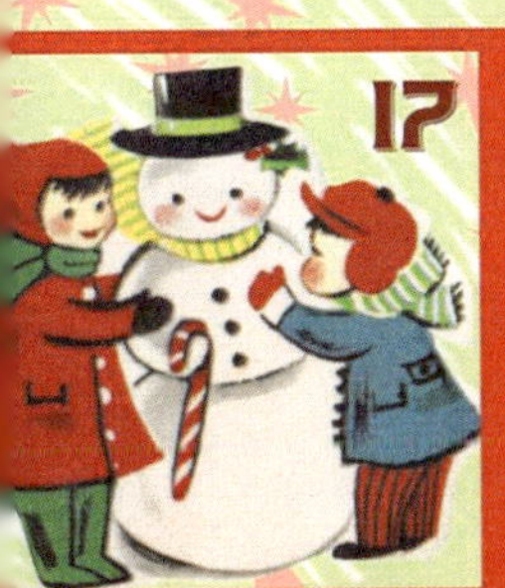

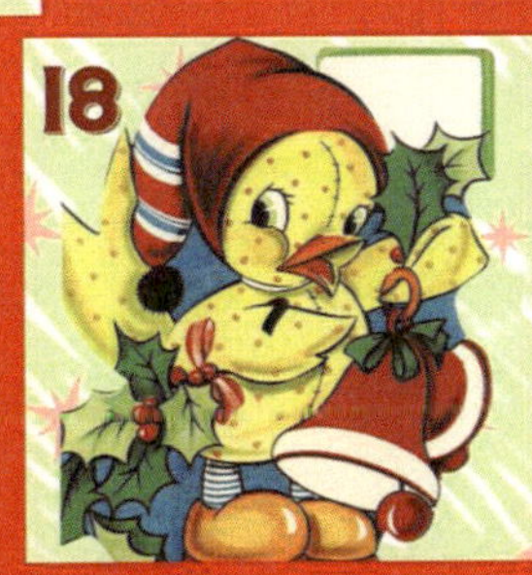
JOY
12

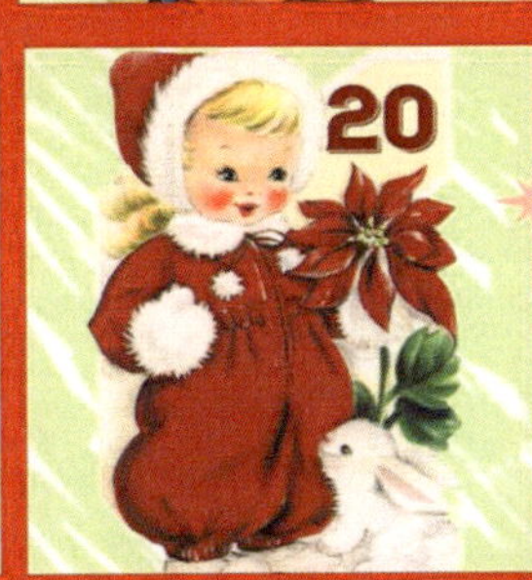
Joy to the World
JOY TO THE WORLD / THE LORD IS
COME: LET EARTH RECEIVE HER KING,
LET EV'RY HEART
PRE-PARE HIM ROOM.
13

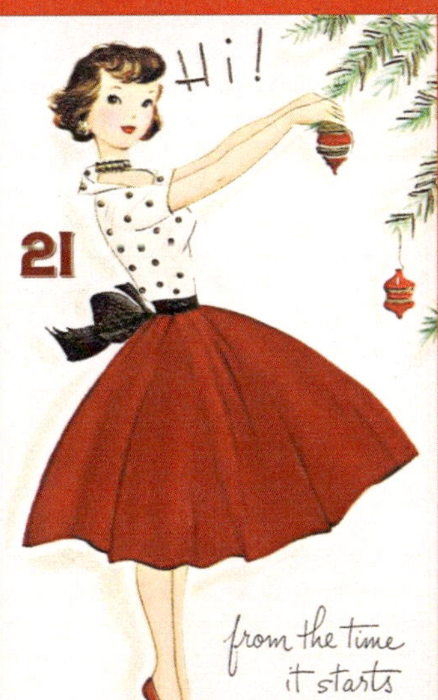
14

15

16

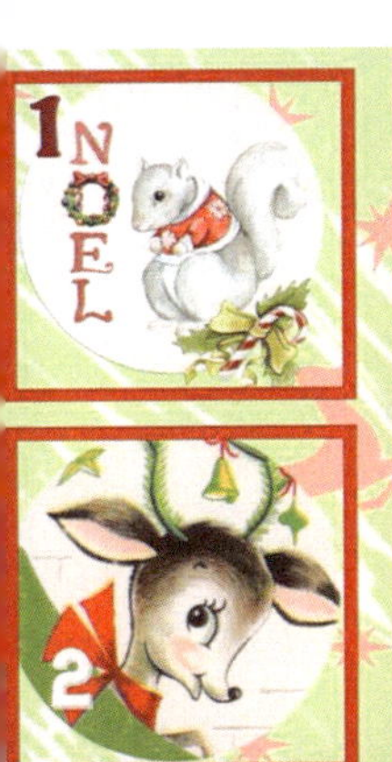
NOEL

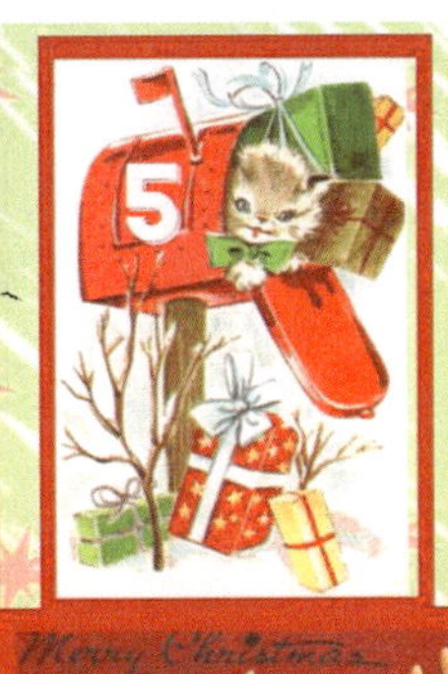
MERRY CHRISTMAS
OOKING FOR SANTA

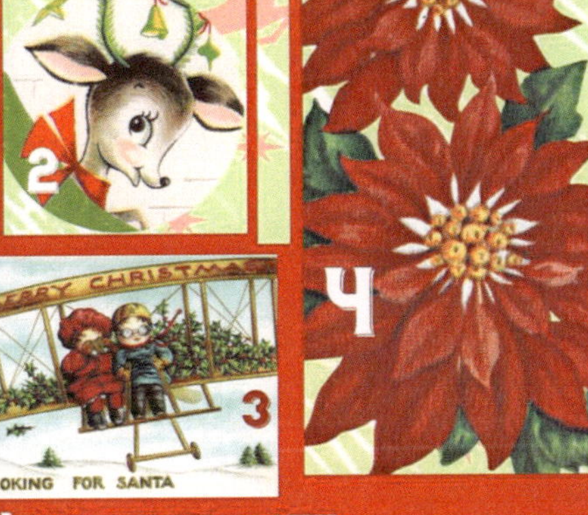

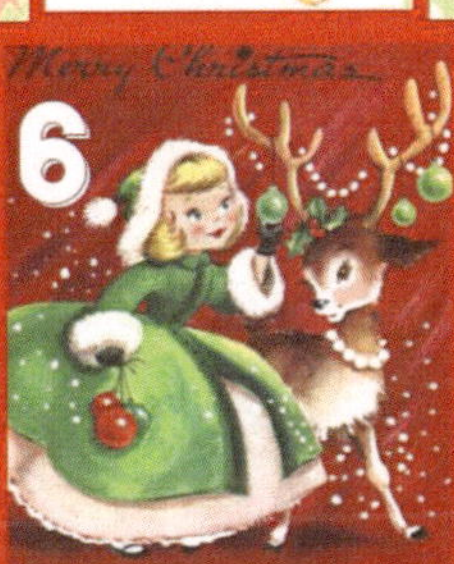

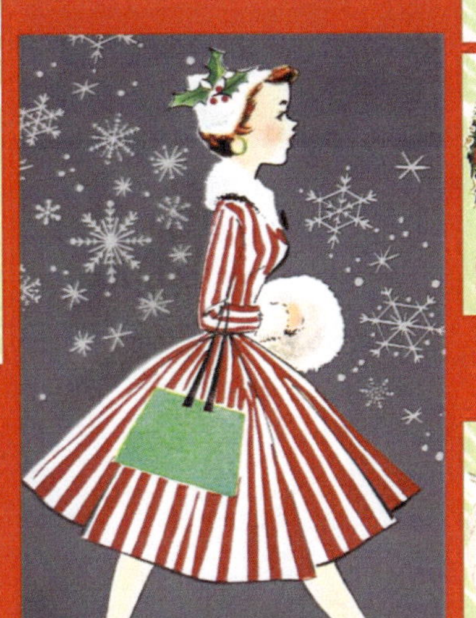
Merry Christmas

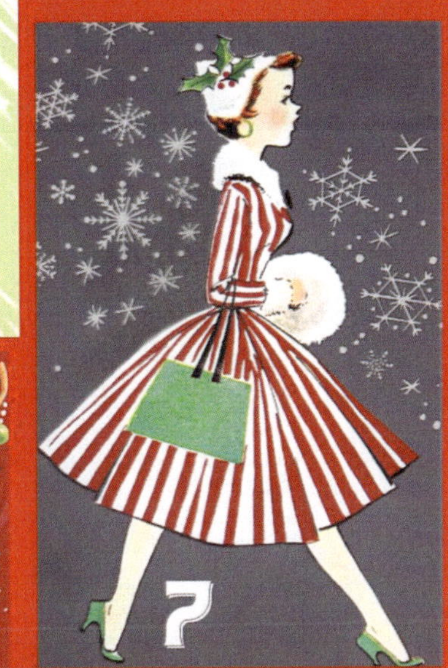

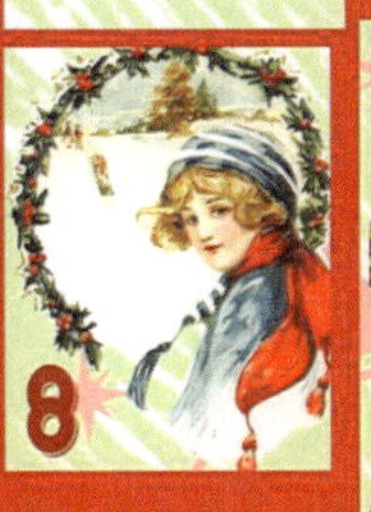

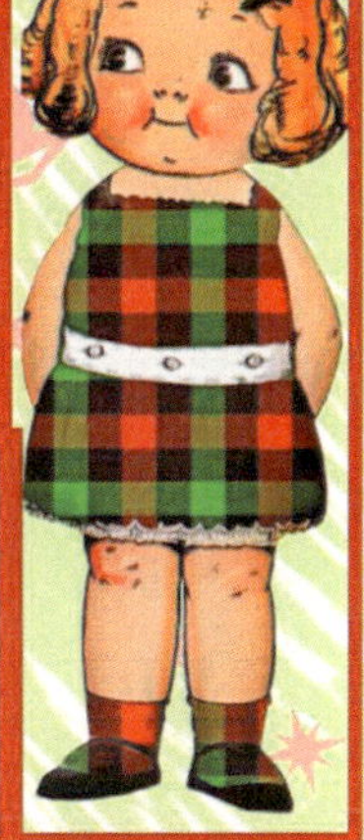

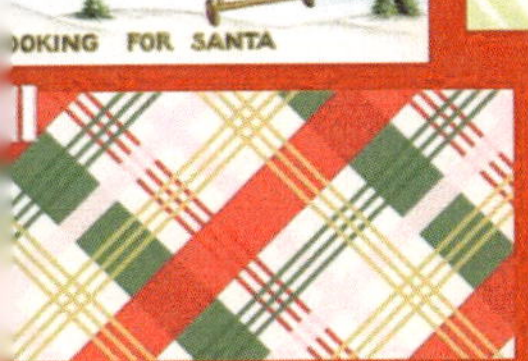

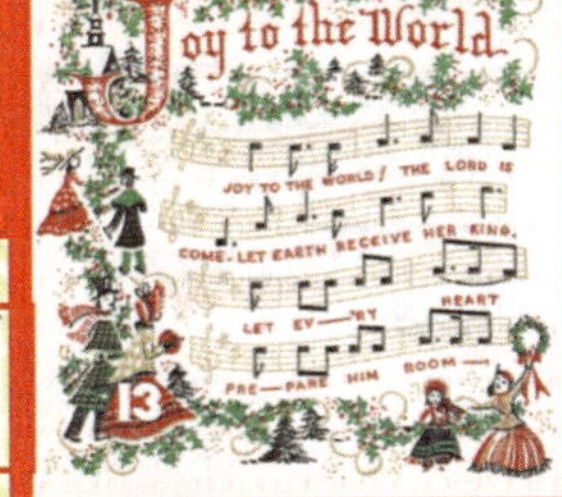
JOY

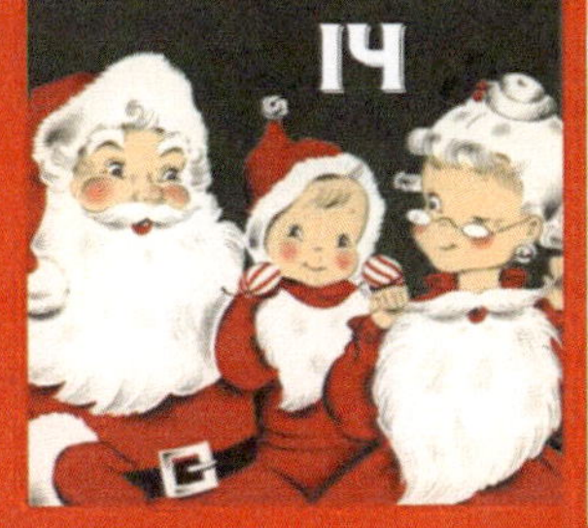
Joy to the World
JOY TO THE WORLD! THE LORD IS
COME. LET EARTH RECEIVE HER KIND,
LET EV'RY HEART
PRE-PARE HIM ROOM

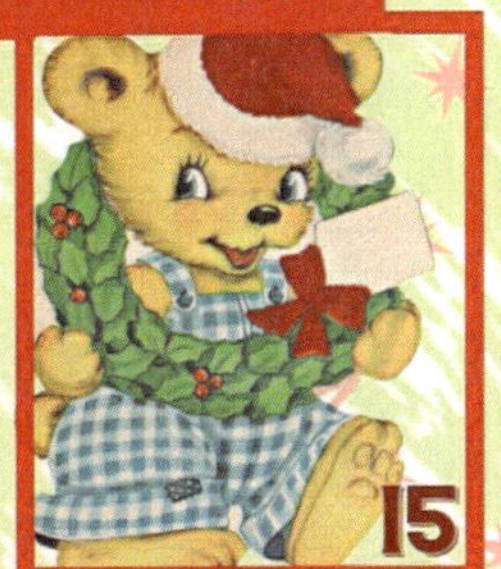

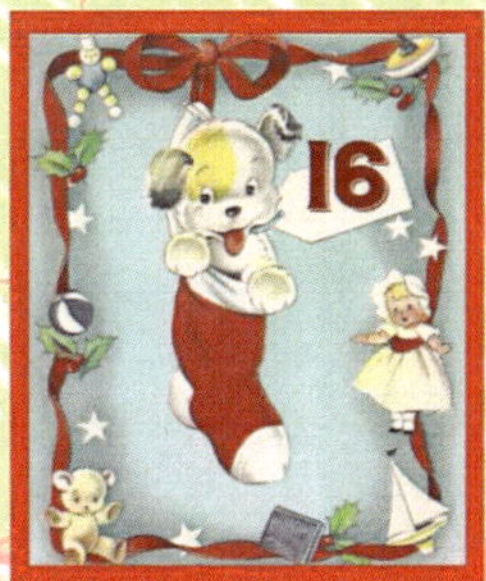

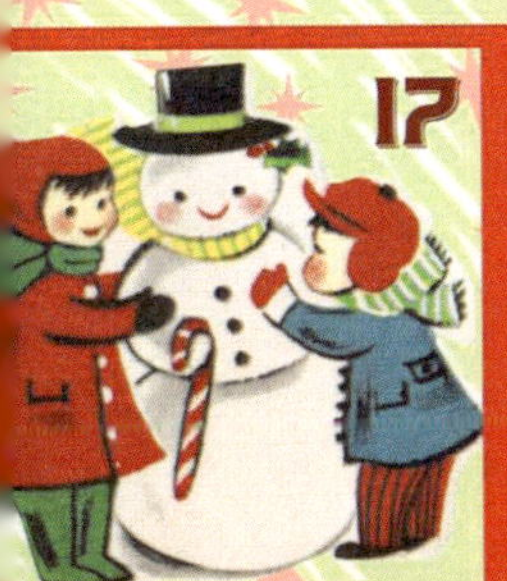

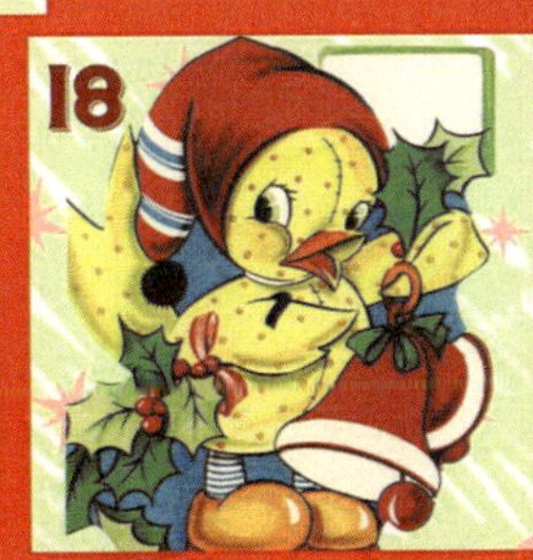

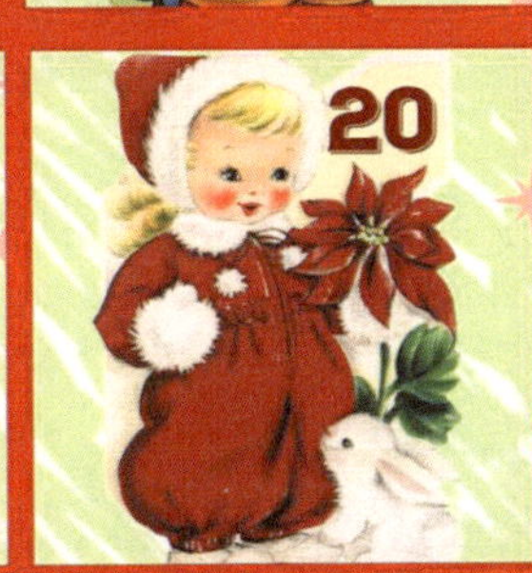

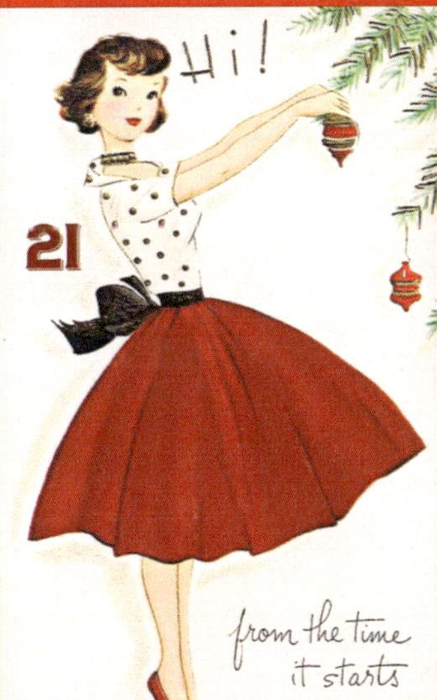
HI!
from the time
it starts

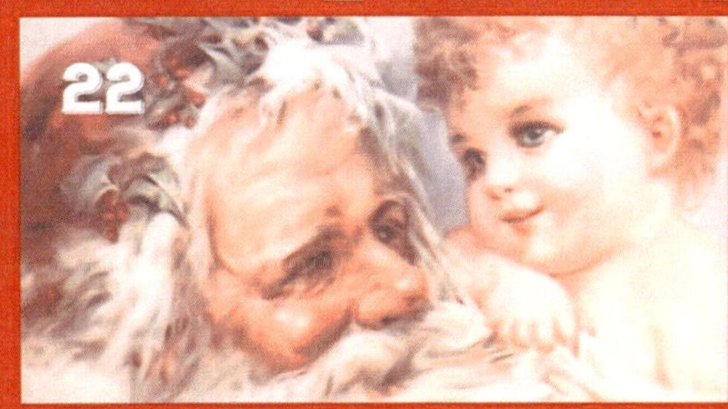

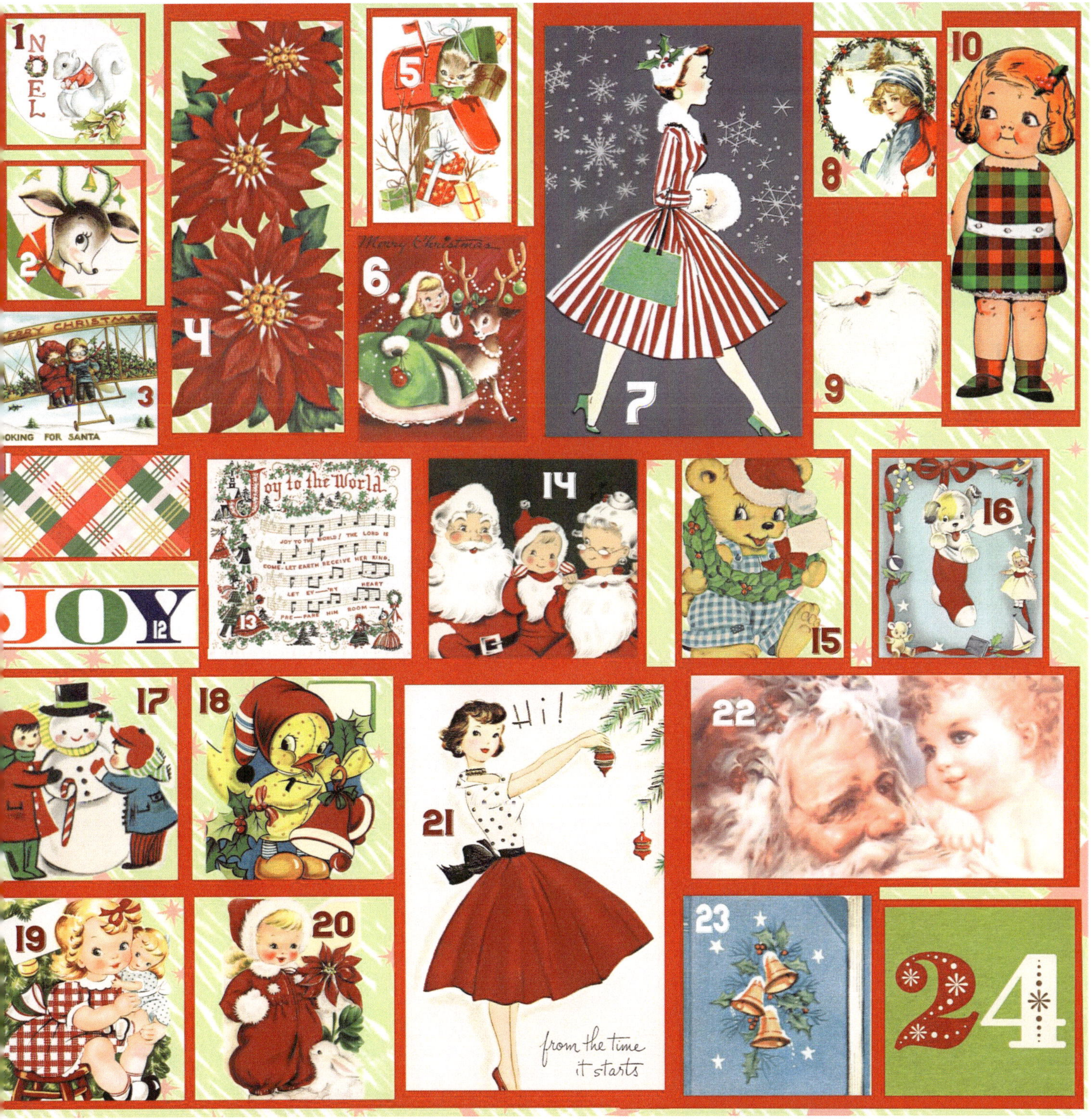

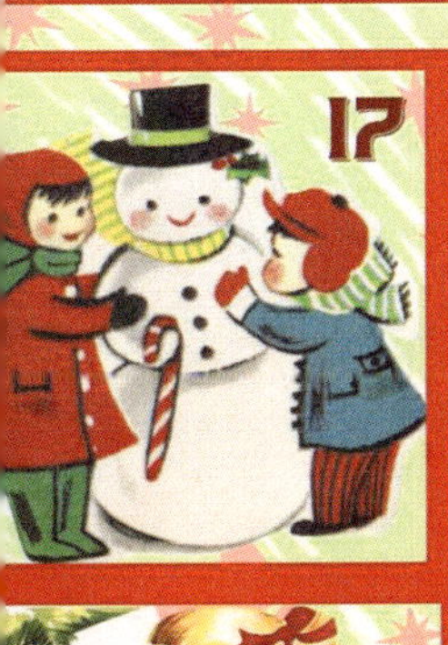
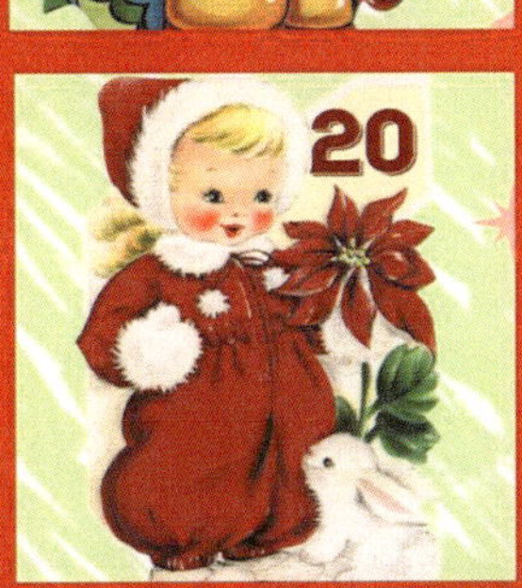
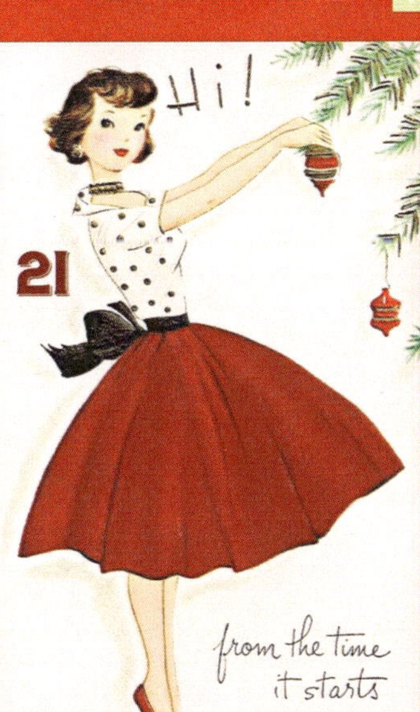
Hi!
21
from the time
it starts

23
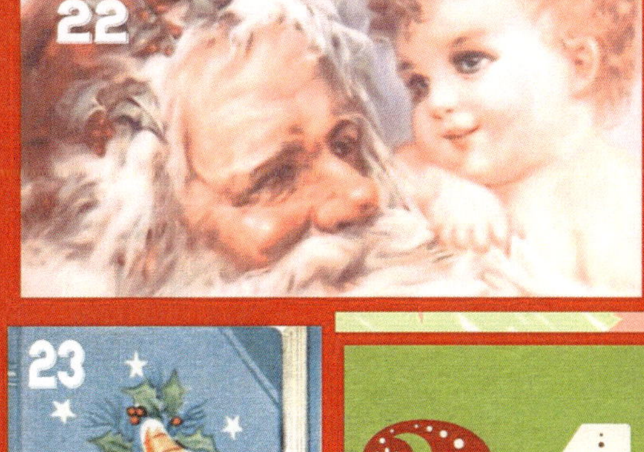
22

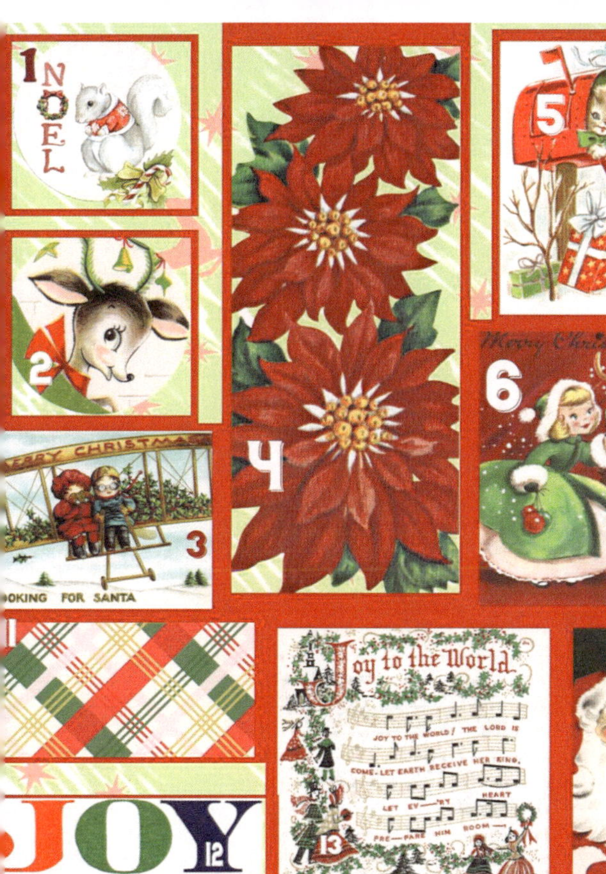
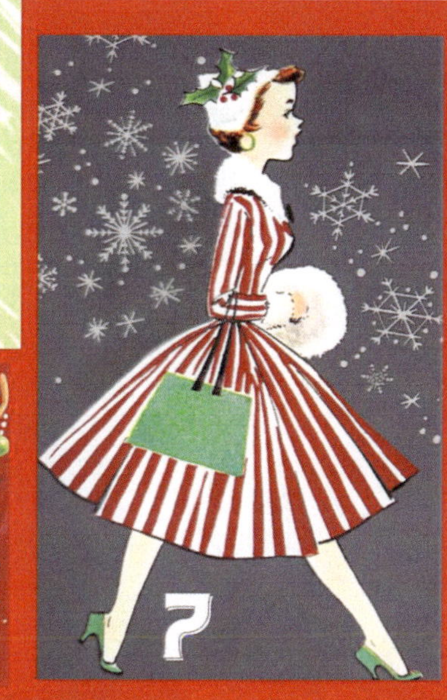
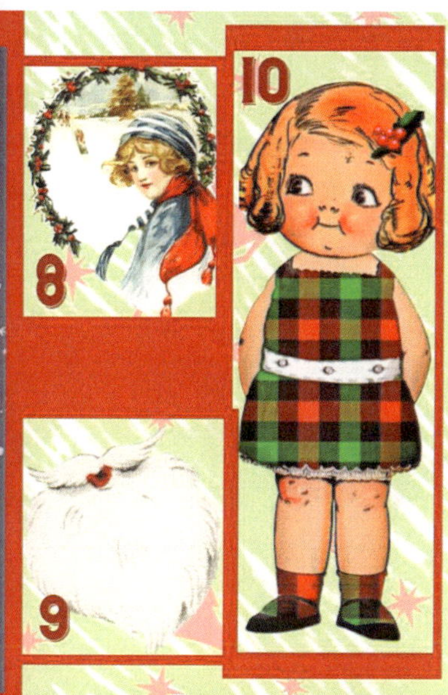
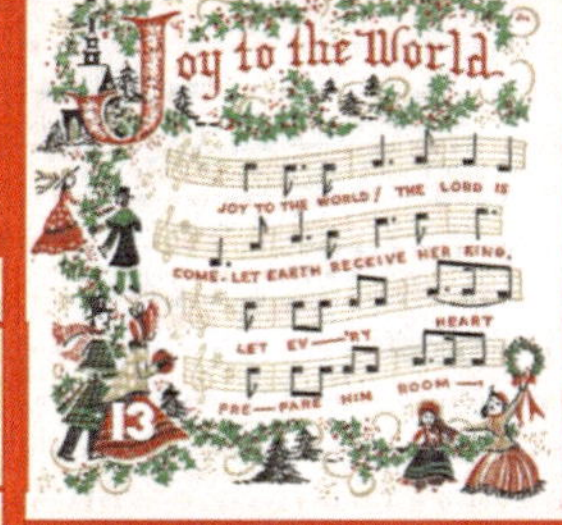
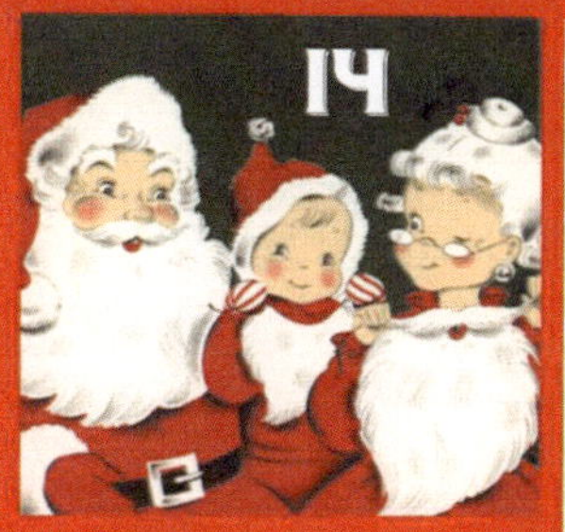
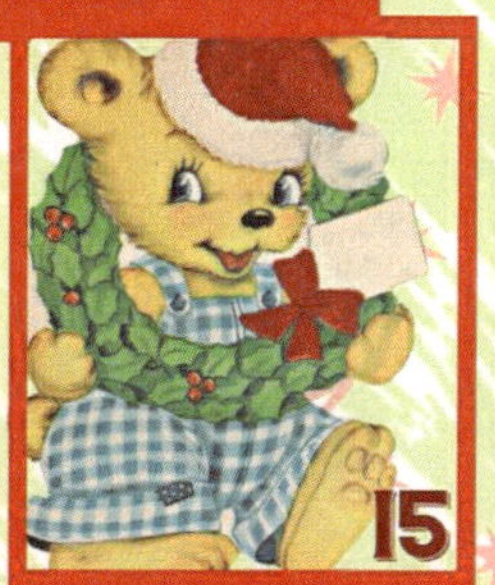
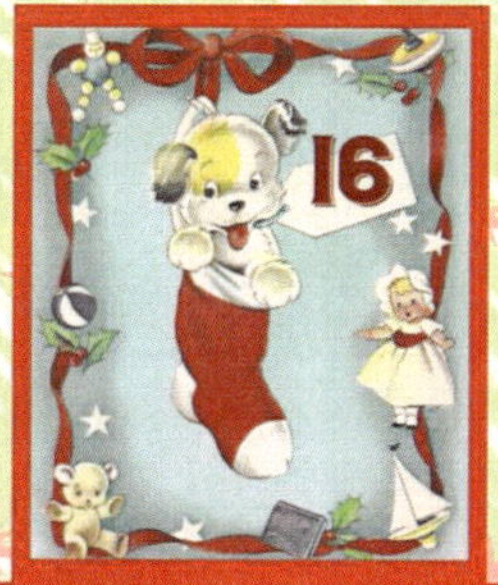
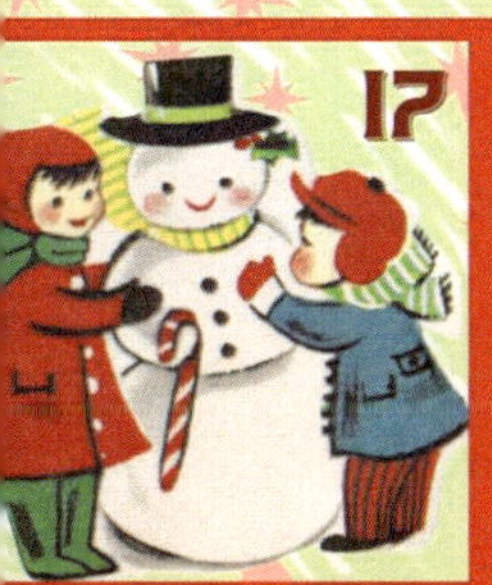
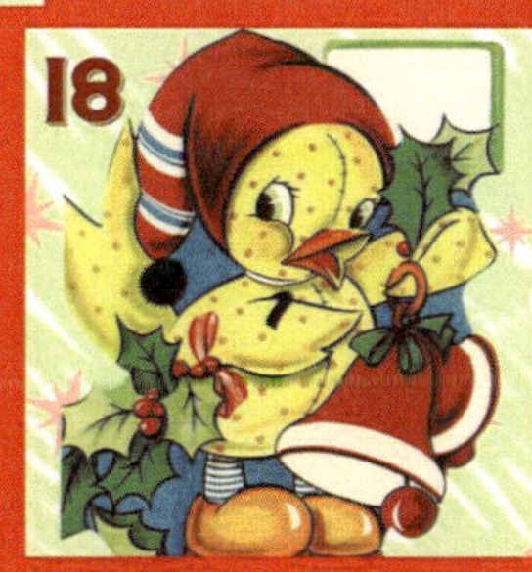
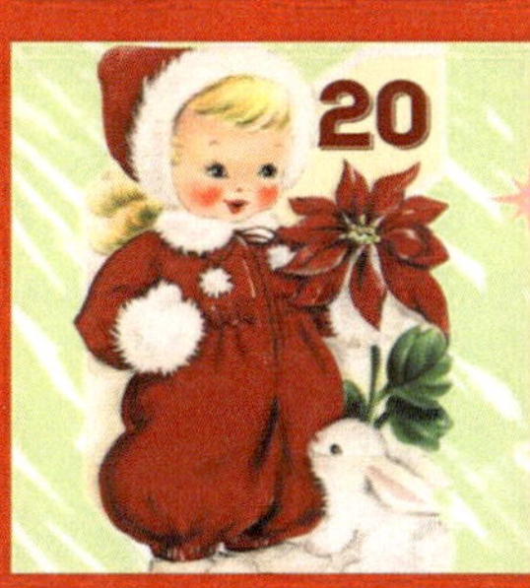
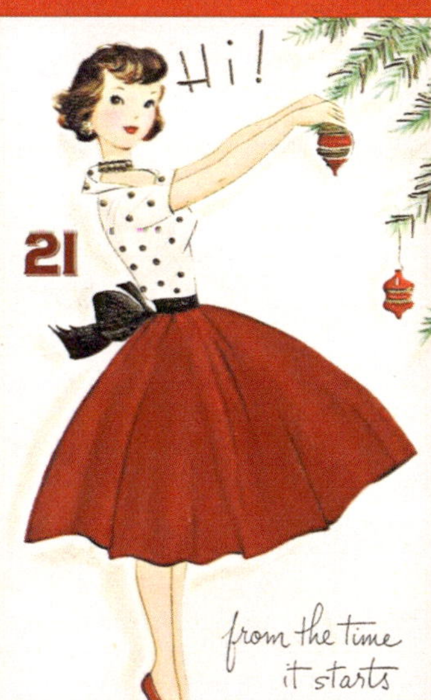
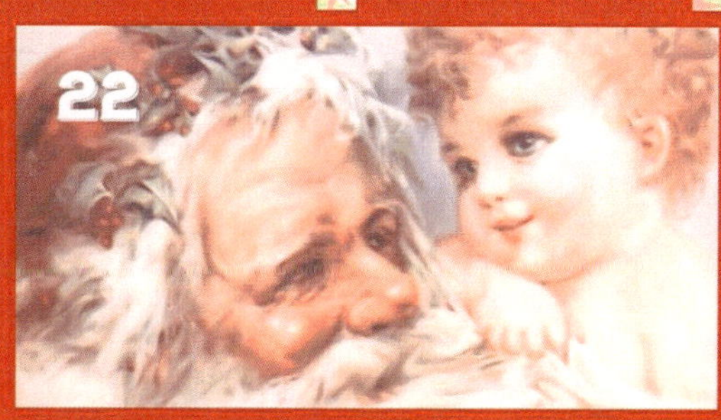

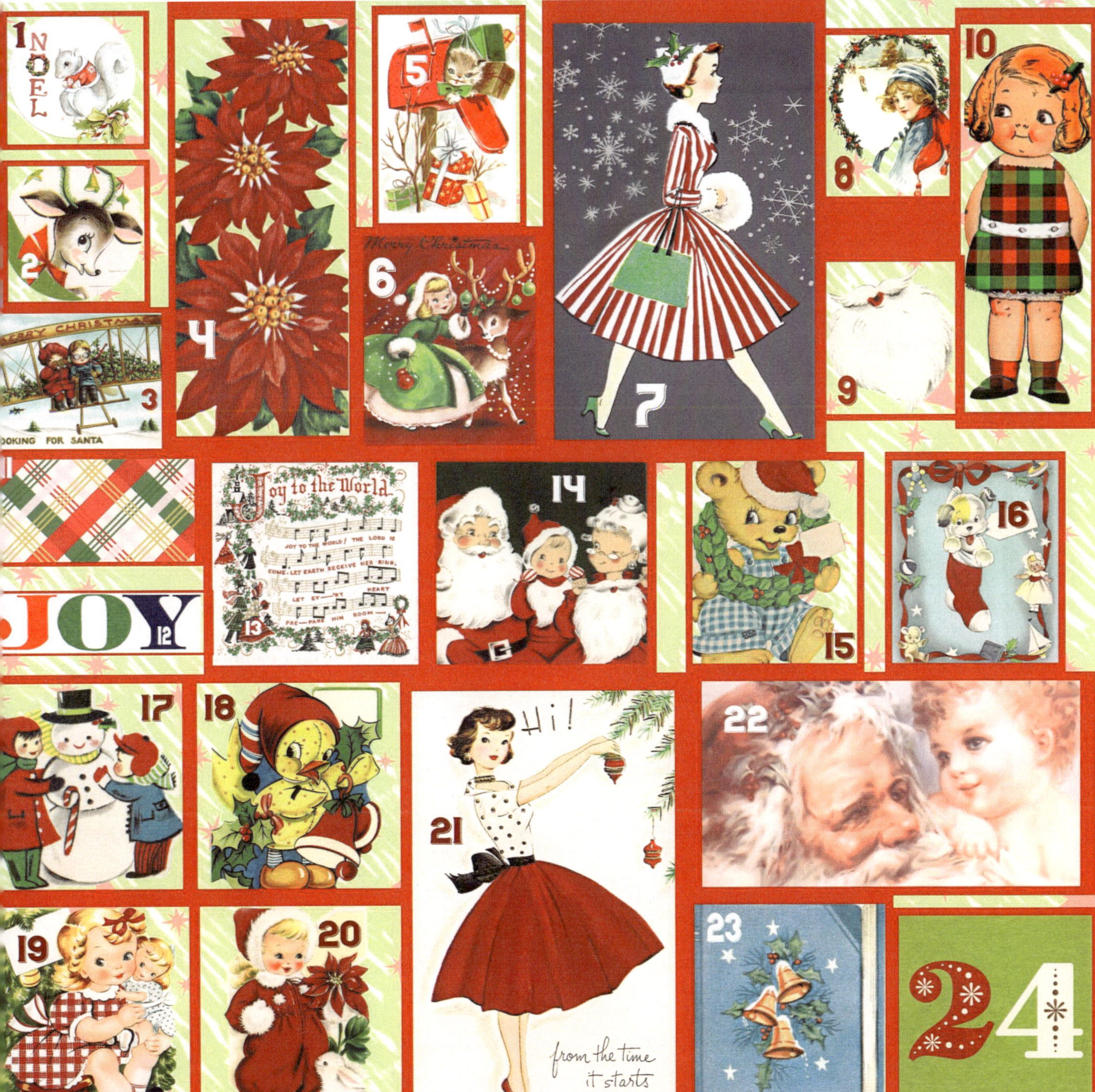

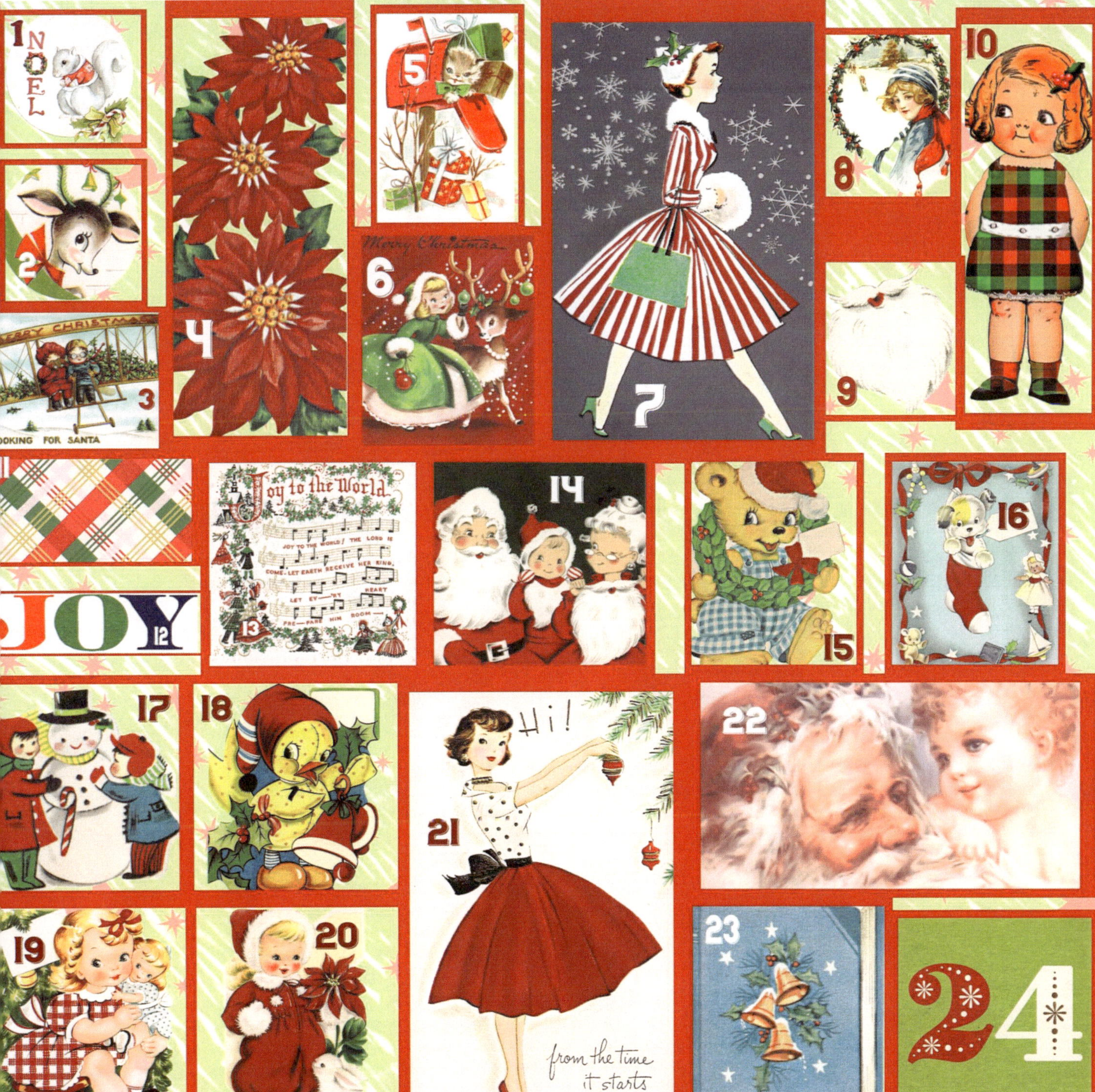

1
NOEL
2
MERRY CHRISTMAS
3
LOOKING FOR SANTA
4
5
Merry Christmas
6
7
8
9
10
JOY to the World
JOY TO THE WORLD / THE LORD IS
COME - LET EARTH RECEIVE HER KING,
LET EV - 'RY HEART
PRE - PARE HIM ROOM
13
JOY
12
14
15
16
17
18
Hi!
21
22
19
20
23
24
from the time
it starts

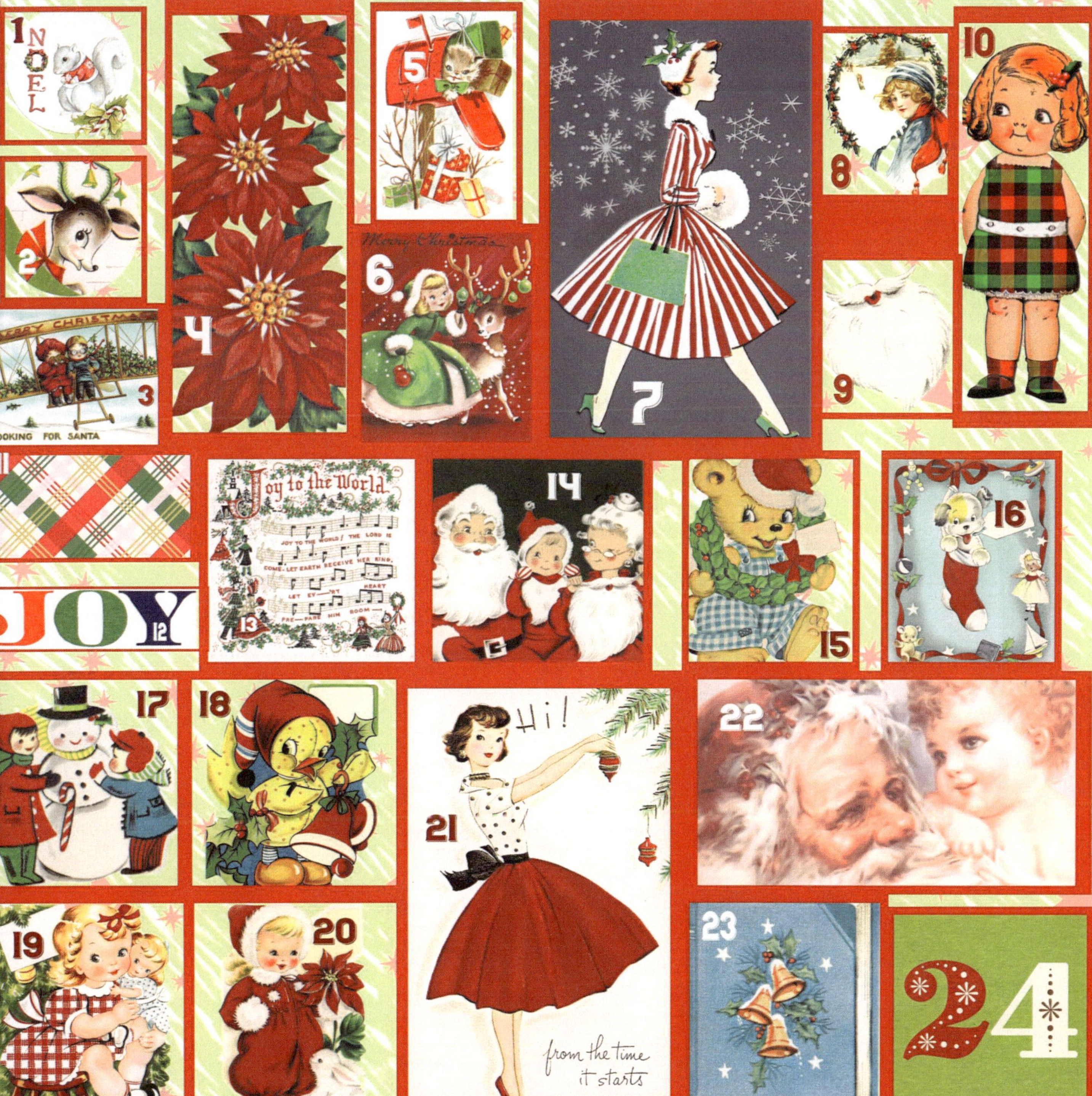

NOEL
MERRY CHRISTMAS
LOOKING FOR SANTA
Merry Christmas
Joy to the World
JOY TO THE WORLD / THE LORD IS
COME LET EARTH RECEIVE HER KIND,
LET EV RY HEART
PRE PARE HIM ROOM
JOY
Hi!
from the time
it starts

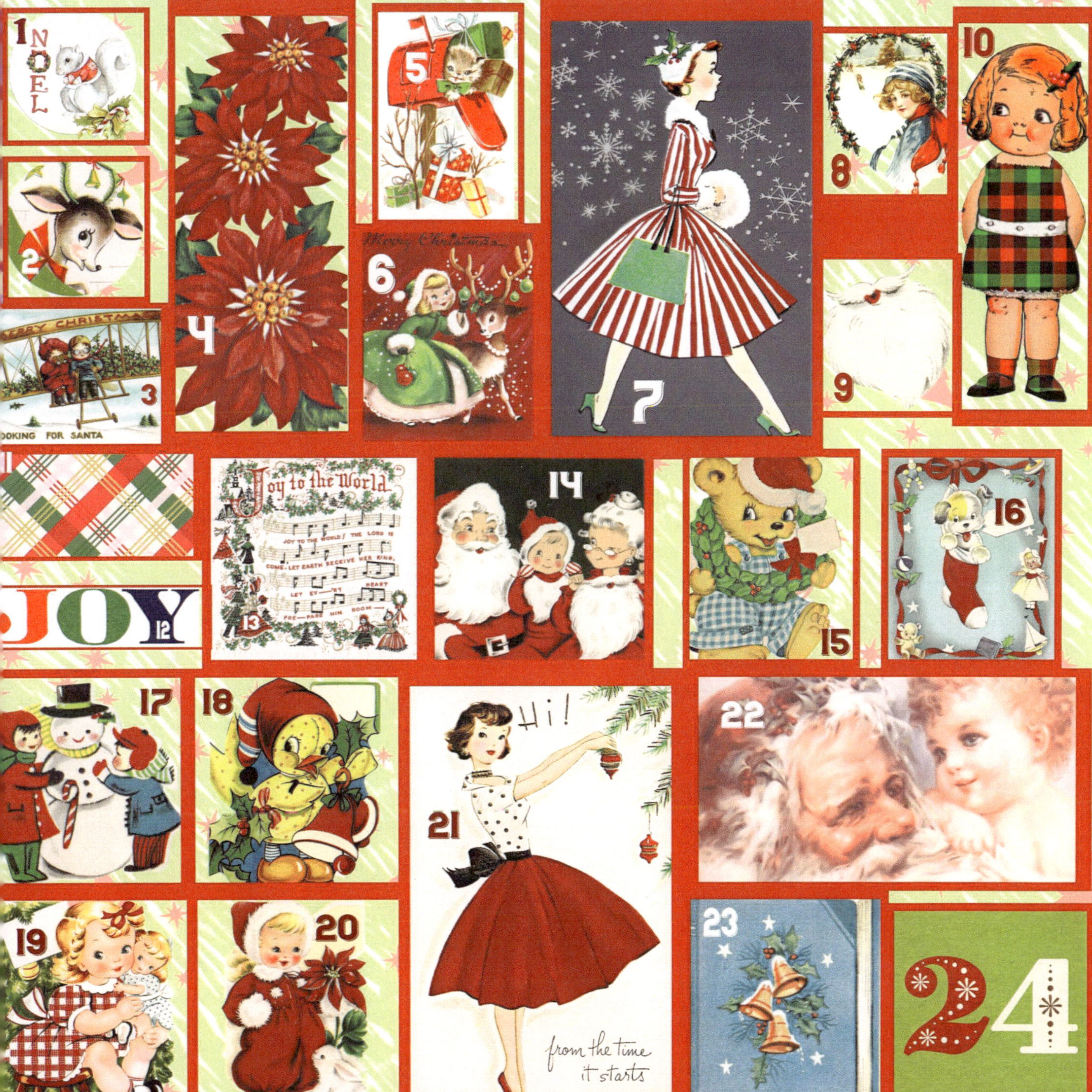
NOEL
LOOKING FOR SANTA
Merry Christmas
Joy to the World
JOY TO THE WORLD / THE LORD IS
COME; LET EARTH RECEIVE HER KING,
LET EV - 'RY HEART
PRE - PARE HIM ROOM.
JOY
HI!
from the time
it starts